LIFE WORKS!

# EXPRESS YOURSELF

## HOW TO HARNESS CREATIVITY

by Sloane Hughes

BEARPORT PUBLISHING

Minneapolis, Minnesota

**Credits:** 6, © Imgorthand/iStock, © A3pfamily/Shutterstock, © MillaF/Shutterstock; 7, © AfricaImages/iStock; 8, © aquatti/Shutterstock; 12, © PIKSEL/iStock; 16, © Lorado/iStock; 19, © Panda Vector/Shutterstock, © vectorplus/Shutterstock; 20, © Fat Camera/iStock, © Alena Ozerova/Shutterstock; 21, © pinstock/iStock; 22, © Samuel Borges Photography/Shutterstock, Ground Picture/Shutterstock; 23, © Ground Picture/Shutterstock, © Yummy Buum/Shutterstock.

**Bearport Publishing Company Product Development Team**
President: Jen Jenson; Director of Product Development: Spencer Brinker; Managing Editor: Allison Juda; Associate Editor: Naomi Reich; Senior Designer: Colin O'Dea; Associate Designer: Elena Klinkner; Associate Designer: Kayla Eggert; Product Development Specialist: Anita Stasson

Library of Congress Cataloging-in-Publication Data is available at www.loc.gov or upon request from the publisher.

ISBN: 979-8-88509-966-0 (hardcover)
ISBN: 979-8-88822-143-3 (paperback)
ISBN: 979-8-88822-286-7 (ebook)



For more information, write to Bearport Publishing, 5357 Penn Avenue South, Minneapolis, MN 55419.

# CONTENTS

# UNIQUE US

We're all different. Big or small, old or young, we each see the world in our own way.

How can we share our **unique** points of view with others? We can **express** ourselves!

# DOING IT DIFFERENTLY

Expressing ourselves can be **creative**. We use our **imaginations** to think differently. What can happen when we do?

We may find new ways to solve problems.

We can think outside the box.

We could come up with brand-new ideas!

When was the last time you used your imagination?

# COMING TOGETHER

Creativity helps us share who we are. It can show how we feel, what we think, and how we see the world. We can express ourselves by writing, drawing, or making music.

We can also learn about others when they are creative. Sharing with creativity and imagination helps us understand one another better.

# SHARE IT

Get creative about something you love with someone you love!

## TRY IT:

### ALL TOGETHER NOW

1. Team up with a friend, and think of something you both like.
2. Then, each make your own piece of art, story, or dance based on that thing.
3. When you are both done, share what you made.
4. Have fun learning about the different things you created!

I made up a snot dance.
I drew a snot monster!

# WHAT IF?

When we get creative, we don't have to do things the same way. Think of something new. Change is good. We can let ourselves go a little crazy!

Try taking a different point of view!

Take a different **approach** to the same old thing. What happens when we look at things in a new way?

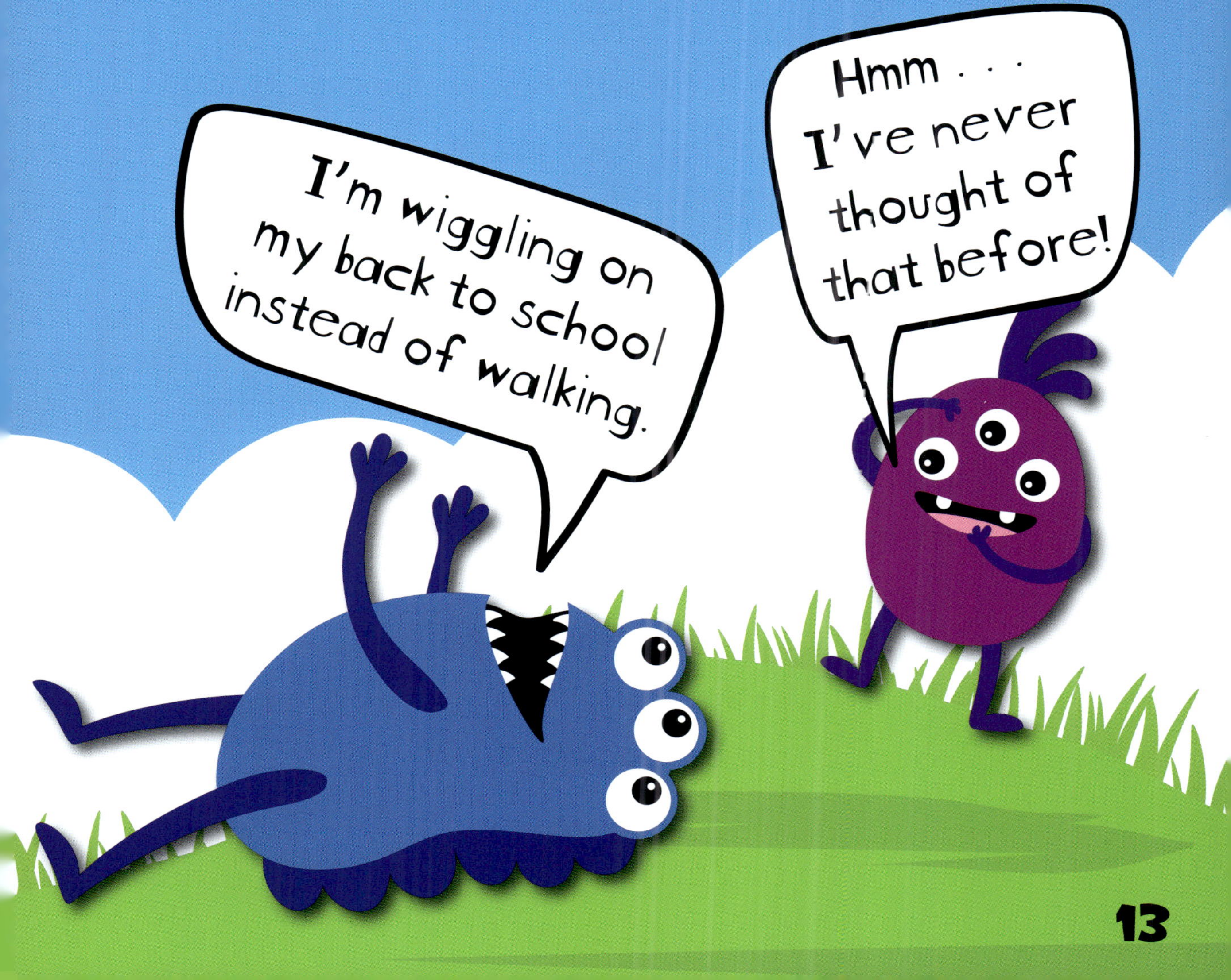

# STORYTELLING

Get creative as you tell a wild and wacky story in a new way!

## TRY IT:

### ONCE UPON A TIME

1. Sit in a circle with a small group of friends.
2. Take turns telling a story together. One person starts with the first sentence.
3. After that, each person gets a turn to add one sentence at a time.
4. Feel free to make your story wacky. How crazy creative can you get?

There was a very hairy monster.
This monster had a fuzzy pet.
Roar!

# INTO THE FLOW

Sometimes, we can get into a **flow**, and it becomes easier for us to make and do things. This easy feeling can help us **focus**.

Some people feel flow when they are playing their favorite sport.

Learning to focus will make it easier to create. We pay attention to what we want. Then, nothing can stop us!

# FEEL THE CREATIVITY

See if you can get creative moving to your favorite song. Can you keep your body in flow?

## TRY IT:

### DANCE IT OUT

1. Turn on your favorite song.
2. Start dancing. See if you can keep moving.
3. Try your best to make each dance move change smoothly into the next one.
4. When the song ends, try a new one!

Look at your flow!
I'm doing the worm!

# CREATIVE EVERY DAY

Being creative can mean trying new things. Sometimes, this feels a bit silly or odd. But when we're open to new ways, anything can happen!

Taking a new path can help us think differently.

Some people like to be creative by themselves.

Working with others can spark creativity.

The more we do it, the easier it can be. Try to be creative every day!

Have you tried something new or done something differently today?

# EXPRESS YOURSELF!

We can do so much when we're creative. We share what we think about the world.

Being creative can help us solve problems. And we may even discover new things! All we need to do is express ourselves.

# GLOSSARY

**approach** a way of coming to or doing something

**creative** able to make new things and ideas

**express** to share something you think or feel

**flow** a feeling where everything is coming easily

**focus** to give your full attention to something

**imaginations** the things that let us think up ideas and act creatively

**unique** special and unlike anything else

# INDEX